"The true competitive advantage in today's gig economy and race to incorporate artificial intelligence into corporate business systems is to unleash the full potential of all human assets. *Safe Enough to Soar* unlocks the key to ineffective team interactions and presents a compelling concept of interaction safety that is the accelerant to effective change management and continuous improvement."

—Marty Belle, Vice President, Global Talent Acquisition and Inclusion & Diversity, W. W. Grainger, Inc.

"Written with clarity and generosity of spirit, this book is urgently needed to help leaders drive organizational success."

—Katrina S. Rogers, PhD, President, Fielding Graduate University

"Accept the invitation of Fred and Judith to be safe enough to soar and learn about the journey to create safe interactions and trust in life and your organization. Their latest work reveals how to transform fear to safety and leverage conflict and disagreement into trust, opportunity, and improved organizational performance. This is a must-read for those seeking to tap the talent, knowledge, and commitment of the people in their organizations."

—James N. Baldwin, JD, EdD, President, Excelsior College

"Through *Safe Enough to Soar*, we are now provided with direction and the context within which to apply the 4 Keys. The book offers a clear pathway through four levels of interaction safety, helping me visualize a route leading to interaction safety as a way of life."

—Andrew Van Breugel, General Manager and Operations Director, Salisbury Operations, Australia, Mayne Pharma International Pty. Ltd.

"Trust. Inclusion. Collaboration. Beyond buzzwords, Fred and Judith outline a process by which organizations can tap into employees' best efforts and thinking. *Safe Enough to Soar* is an invitation for everyone to create environments at work that foster real engagement and contribution."

—Tony Bingham, President and CEO, Association for Talent Development

"What a timely time . . . to prod and push us, aspirationally and pragmatically, to consider and to embrace a new level of connecting with each other to benefit individuals and organizations!

Your competence and dedication across decades to create safe and powerful interactions for all is much appreciated."
—**Joseph C. High, former Senior Vice President and Chief People Officer, W. W. Grainger, Inc.**

"In today's challenging and ever-changing work environments, interaction safety is crucial for individuals and organizations to reach their full potential and soar. Fred and Judith provide a visionary and practical guide for how to achieve it as a way of life."
—**Mary-Frances Winters, founder and CEO, The Winters Group, Inc.**

"Interaction safety levels bring to life the courageous journey people are on in society today. As businesses move to Level Four, skyrocketing employee engagement will drive out organizational waste, and businesses will see tremendous growth."
—**Kathy Clements, former Vice President, Lean Six Sigma, Ecolab**

"*Safe Enough to Soar* seamlessly weaves together complex concepts of systems thinking, the business case for culture change, and neuroscience in a simple and engaging yet highly effective format."
—**Deb Dagit, President, Deb Dagit Diversity, and former Vice President and Chief Diversity Officer, Merck**

"Judith and Fred provide what participants, students, and my executive clients all ask for: How do I create enough safety in my workplace to fully engage people and put the tough issues out openly on the table?"
—**Robert J. Marshak, PhD, author of *Covert Processes at Work***

"Typically in government, the workforce is the constant and leadership is viewed by the workforce as temporary. The mentality of 'I'll still be here after they are gone' is difficult to break through. Political influence is strong and allies are hard to find. Fred and Judith's ability to identify the current state and simply lay out a plan for change provides leadership with a road map to promote cultural change in an environment that is somewhat intolerant of it. Their insight and knowledge gained from a multitude of organizations and experiences provide workplace scenarios applicable to every environment."
—**Monica Kurzejeski, Deputy Mayor, City of Troy, New York**

"As a woman business founder and owner, I know firsthand what it means to be able to speak out and speak up. As a business leader, I recognize that creating an environment that supports all individuals to be their best self, contribute fully, and learn openly from others is a model not only for our companies but for our society as well."

—**Lynne Katzmann, founder and CEO, Juniper Communities**

"An important new book about an important new understanding of safety in the workplace. *Safe Enough to Soar* is an easy read that calls out a complex organizational challenge. The authors' definition of interaction safety is clear, and the four levels of safety they describe are accessible and understandable. The key to this book is the value it provides to organizations of all types by challenging us all to do better by ourselves, our colleagues, and our workplaces."

—**Steve Humerickhouse, Executive Director, The Forum on Workplace Inclusion**

"Miller and Katz have elevated safety as a key condition in creating inclusive cultures in their model of interaction safety. Safety is often in the eyes of the beholder. The four levels of safety described are critical for people to explore, examine, and enact to assess not only how safe *they* feel but also how they *contribute to creating a culture of safety for others*. Miller and Katz offer concrete examples to make cultures that are more than safe enough to soar!"

—**Ilene Wasserman, PhD, President, ICW Consulting Group**

"When we rolled out the 4 Keys to collaboration (from the same authors), we spent a surprising amount of time on the themes that are captured and addressed in this book. I can therefore recommend it for stand-alone initiatives aimed at helping employees speak up, speak out, and be heard, as well as for use before, during, or after deployment of the 4 Keys."

—**Mike Ali, PhD, former CIO, W. W. Grainger, Inc.**

"How do we create a great work environment where people feel safe to be fully involved and able to do their best work? Fred and Judith offer a highly engaging, thoughtful, and much-needed way to establish interaction safety so people can offer both their best and still-forming ideas."

—**John Vogelsang, PhD, Editor-in-Chief, *OD Practitioner*, Organization Development Network, and Director, Michael Harrington Center, Queens College, City University of New York**

"Just finished reading the book and wanted to let you know how moved I am by the message and your crystal-clear view of what

inclusion can look like when intentionally practiced and authentically experienced."
—Plácida V. Gallegos, PhD, President, Solfire Consulting LLC

"For leaders, this book provides a much-needed, practical road map for creating a work environment where everyone feels safe to speak up and challenge the status quo. The four levels of interaction safety, enhanced with checklists and relevant examples, demystify the steps toward realizing a culture of candidness, trust, and inclusion."
—Monica E. Biggs, EdD, independent OD consultant

"If you want to create a work environment that brings out the best in people and fosters collaboration and respect, *Safe Enough to Soar* is the place to start. The concept of interaction safety is a powerful tool to diagnose and remedy the negative interpersonal dynamics that typically stifle workplaces. Great ideas come out of creative conflict; this book is an illuminating and practical guide to transforming your workplace into an environment where that creativity can be realized."
—Christopher Ames, PhD, President, The Sage Colleges

"This book will be an essential part of the toolkit for everyone who wants to learn how to make inclusion part of our everyday reality. When all those in organizations take the message of this book to heart and integrate its lessons into their behavior, relationships, and work, we will have gone a long way to achieving the benefits of inclusion."
—Bernardo M. Ferdman, PhD, Distinguished Professor Emeritus, California School of Professional Psychology; Principal, Ferdman Consulting; and editor of *Diversity at Work*

"Powerful concepts and building blocks for enhancing engagement and a sense of belonging."
—Effenus Henderson, Codirector, Institute for Sustainable Diversity and Inclusion

"The journey from Level One to Level Four, is directly linked to creating a distinct competitive advantage via the collective insight of a motivated and fully engaged workforce, . . . which allows individuals to bring all their ideas and concerns, without fear of criticism or critique, unleashing the power of the whole organization."
—Victor Lusvardi, Market Development Director, The Chemours Company

"Many have decried the tendency for organizations to encourage difficult conversations or robust dialogue without due regard for the lack of interaction safety in those conversations. I have not come across many books that address this topic with such clarity like Fred and Judith have done. I am particularly drawn to their definition that interaction safety includes not only the feelings of safety to share best ideas but their still-in-formation ideas. It is only when we feel free to speak that we can share ideas that are still in formation—where we do not feel judged and have accepted that everyone can be wrong at times. Interaction safety leads to rich dialogue and creative solutions to problems. Excellent addition to the work of creating inclusive workplaces. Well done!"

—Nene Molefi, author and CEO, Mandate Molefi

"Once again, Fred and Judith bring to light a relevant observation on what people in organizations do that prevents us from becoming our best."

—Randy Wilson, Director, Organizational Development, Pier 1 Imports

"Taking the time to create interactive safety reaps numerous benefits for organizations and allows energies once dedicated to protective measures to be translated to generative and productive outcomes. The four levels of interaction safety are described through a developmental continuum, illustrated through real-life scenarios that readers will find familiar regardless of the professional sector in which one is employed. The definition provided of interaction safety helps the reader understand the behaviors and mindsets necessary for creating a work environment where differences are respected and leveraged and where reasonable risk taking is rewarded."

—Mark A. Puente, Director of Diversity and Leadership Programs, Association of Research Libraries

"Your observation that a lack of personal interaction safety will lead to self-editing of the very communications that could improve an organization's performance is, at once, simple and elegant."

—Francis Murdock Pitts, FAIA, FACHA, OAA, Principal, architecture+

"This book takes readers along a journey from a work environment characterized by judgment, blame, and bullying to one of collaboration, learning, engagement, and contribution."

—Charles Pfeffer, CEO Coach and President, Contextus LLC

"To fully leverage diversity we must foster an environment where people feel safe to show up authentically and give 100 percent of themselves. *Safe Enough to Soar* skillfully outlined four levels of interaction safety and provides a pragmatic process that will help move from D&I strategy to activation."

—Lily C. Prost, Executive Vice President and Chief Human Resources Officer, J. M. Huber Corporation

"What sets Judith and Fred apart as authors is their ability to engage their readers as allies and empower them to make a difference in their organizations."

—Khamel Abdulai, Director of Training, Excelsior College

"*Safe Enough to Soar* is a wonderful extension to Fred and Judith's amazing body of work teaching us how to create inclusive environments where people can bring their full selves to their work each day."

—Rob Guenard, PhD, Senior Director, Biogen

"By creating clear guidelines and pathways for creating safe environments, Fred and Judith have given us a road map for enhancing trust in our relationships and in our organizations and a guidebook for engagement and fulfillment in our daily lives!"

—Howard J. Ross, founder of Cook Ross and author of *Our Search for Belonging*

"For the many individuals who do not feel safe at work—whether they are on the front line or in a leadership role—this book presents a way to name the behaviors and simple methods to work in their organization while maximizing their personal sense of self and interaction safety."

—Leigh Wilkinson, Program Manager, Project Management Office, State of Maine

"Working in a foreign country, I was very skeptical as to how the principles of *Safe Enough to Soar* would actually work. As I began to implement the seven steps to creating interaction safety, I was amazed at how quickly my team adopted the practices, and they have become the norm. I can see not only how our meetings have changed but how much faster solutions are agreed upon, pushing the organization to a higher level. I can say, firsthand, this book transcends geographic and cultural boundaries."

—Cindy Szadokierski, Vice President, Airport Operations, IndiGo

Safe Enough to Soar

SAFE ENOUGH TO SOAR

Accelerating Trust, Inclusion & Collaboration in the Workplace

FREDERICK A. MILLER & JUDITH H. KATZ

**FOREWORDS BY DEBORAH DAGIT
AND HAROLD L. YOH III**

Berrett–Koehler Publishers, Inc.
a BK Business book

Berrett-Koehler Publishers, Inc.
1333 Broadway, Suite 1000
Oakland, CA 94612-1921
Tel: (510) 817-2277
Fax: (510) 817-2278
www.bkconnection.com

ORDERING INFORMATION
Quantity sales. Special discounts are available on quantity purchases by corporations, associations, and others. For details, contact the "Special Sales Department" at the Berrett-Koehler address above.
Individual sales. Berrett-Koehler publications are available through most bookstores. They can also be ordered directly from Berrett-Koehler: Tel: (800) 929-2929; Fax: (802) 864-7626; www.bkconnection.com.
Orders for college textbook / course adoption use. Please contact Berrett-Koehler: Tel: (800) 929-2929; Fax: (802) 864-7626.

Distributed to the U.S. trade and internationally by Penguin Random House Publisher Services.

Berrett-Koehler and the BK logo are registered trademarks of Berrett-Koehler Publishers, Inc.

Printed in Canada

Berrett-Koehler books are printed on long-lasting acid-free paper. When it is available, we choose paper that has been manufactured by environmentally responsible processes. These may include using trees grown in sustainable forests, incorporating recycled paper, minimizing chlorine in bleaching, or recycling the energy produced at the paper mill.

Library of Congress Cataloging-in-Publication Data

Names: Miller, Frederick A., 1946– author. | Katz, Judith H., 1950– author.
Title: Safe enough to soar : accelerating trust, inclusion &
    collaboration in the workplace / Frederick A. Miller, Judith Katz.
Description: First Edition. | Oakland : Berrett-Koehler Publishers, 2018.
Identifiers: LCCN 2018030446 | ISBN 9781523098057 (paperback)
Subjects: LCSH: Teams in the workplace. | Interpersonal relations. |
    Leadership. | Organizational behavior. | BISAC: BUSINESS &
    ECONOMICS / Human Resources & Personnel Management. |
    BUSINESS & ECONOMICS / Organizational Behavior. |
    BUSINESS & ECONOMICS / Workplace Culture.
Classification: LCC HD66 .M54455 2018 | DDC 658.3/82—dc23
LC record available at https://lccn.loc.gov/2018030446

First Edition
25 24 23 22 21 20 19 18   10 9 8 7 6 5 4 3 2 1

Set in 10.5 Stone Serif by Westchester Publishing Services
Text designer: Mimi Heft
Cover designer: Mimi Heft

Clarice Roberta Gaines Miller
22 February 1912–6 January 2018
*My 105-year-old mother, my number-one supporter and someone
I loved dearly, died on 6 January 2018.*

I love the saying, "Parents give you **roots and wings**."
That is what my mother did for me:

ROOTS . . .
In Philly
Pride in being African American
Fully caring about others
Living a respectful life
Working hard
Achieving things

AND WINGS!
All that I have been
All that I am
All that I will be

My life with Mom—a very solid and always-present
foundation for me—is what made me the person I am
today and will be tomorrow.

THANKS, Mom! I love you. Journey well.

—FAM

Dedicated to all the women and men who were brave enough
to speak up! Especially to David Levine, my partner in life;
Edie Seashore, my mentor; and my mom, Ilse Katz—role
models of honesty, authenticity, and courage.

—JHK

Contents

Foreword

Deborah Dagit
President, Deb Dagit Diversity, former vice president and chief diversity officer, Merck

I met Judith and Fred in the early 1990s when the field of diversity and inclusion was being shaped by forward-thinking companies and practitioners. They have been innovative thought leaders and patient mentors and teachers, and there are thousands of us who have benefited from their insights. As chief diversity officer for more than twenty years in three companies that were recognized as trailblazers in diversity and inclusion, I looked to their guidance to make the complex simple when developing and implementing enterprise-wide strategies. I was also fortunate to work with them when they led a project at Merck in our global manufacturing division to help transform the business, utilizing many of the principles in *Safe Enough to Soar*.

Safety has a slightly different meaning in my life. I am the height and weight of a six-year-old due to a genetic condition I was born with that causes brittle bones. An exercise Judith and Fred use illustrates my hyperawareness of physical environments. They show a sidewalk and ask what people notice first. Leaping out of the picture for me were the uneven sections that could result in a fracture. I am also acutely aware of how people experience me as a leader. When we first meet, they often express feelings of emotional vulnerability and fear that they will do or say the "wrong thing" due to the novelty of interacting with any "little person," much less one in an influential and visible executive role. These teachable moments are part of my life every day.

Safety, belonging, and trust are key ingredients for a workplace culture that aspires to delight customers and create and deliver innovative products. In *Safe Enough to Soar*, authentic stories of real people and situations illustrate the key points, and the checklists for individuals and managers point the way to creating a high-functioning culture of inclusion. I recommend utilizing this memorable and practical resource.

Foreword

Harold L. Yoh III
Chair and CEO, Day & Zimmermann

I am honored that Fred and Judith asked me to write a foreword for their new book. I've known both of them for many years. Fred serves on Day & Zimmermann's board of advisers, and Fred and Judith have helped change our culture to allow our people to feel "safe enough to soar." As an introduction to my work life, since 1999, I have been chair and CEO of Day & Zimmermann, a century-old, family-owned company. Our workforce is over forty-three thousand strong.

At Day & Zimmermann, our number-one value is safety. We feel that we have a world-class safety culture in which people look after each other, point out safety hazards, and make sure they are fixed. We constantly ask, "Why not zero?"

Witnessing someone getting hurt gives us a sick feeling inside. We wonder about the individual's recovery. We feel concern for his or her family and coworkers. We ask how we are going to prevent similar instances from happening in the future. We never want injuries to happen—we truly believe that all accidents are preventable.

So we ask, "Why not zero interaction issues?" We set the bar high. We believe it's achievable, and the principles in Fred and Judith's new book have equipped us with the tools to soar to success.

This book takes you through the four levels of interaction safety. Fred and Judith show the way to transform your workplace to make interaction safety a way of life. At Level Four, people are engaged through voicing their thoughts, challenging each other's points of view, and building on each other's ideas. The workplace at Level Four is a place where everyone feels valued and respected. Creating this trusting organization allows quicker decisions and implementations.

In competitive business landscapes, we win when we bring the best solution to our clients' needs. In a workplace where everyone feels "safe enough to soar," innovation will flourish.

Thank you, Fred and Judith, for sharing your ideas on interaction safety and creating a road map to guide people to be themselves and be their best.

Welcome to
Safe Enough to Soar

We need safety in our interactions now more than ever.

Organizations need people to speak up about issues that get in the way of their ability to perform at their best. Greater interdependency among organizational units requires more collaborative interactions to innovate, solve problems, and make decisions organizations need to achieve their goals.

We would like to report that most organizations recognize the importance of creating greater levels of interaction safety in their workplaces, but our experience suggests otherwise:

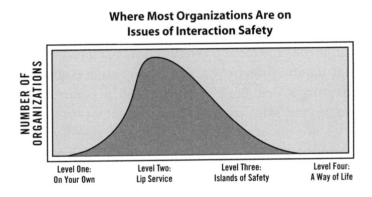

Where Most Organizations Are on Issues of Interaction Safety

NUMBER OF ORGANIZATIONS

Level One: On Your Own | Level Two: Lip Service | Level Three: Islands of Safety | Level Four: A Way of Life

Some organizations pay a great deal of attention to ensuring the physical safety of their team members. We believe it is vital to add interaction safety to the way people in organizations think about the work environment. This creates an environment in which people feel safe enough to be their best selves and

- don't feel as though they must walk on eggshells, stay within narrow boundaries, or worry about being judged
- freely share their ideas and engage with others
- feel valued, respected, and able to do their best work
- challenge each other's point of view
- express their differences and similarities
- to be brave

. . . a workplace where individuals can feel fully included and soar.

In other words, adding interaction safety creates a winning, growing, inspiring, and self-sustaining environment in which people achieve more together than they would alone. It opens doors to accelerating trust, inclusion, and collaboration in the workplace.

Please don't misunderstand. What we are describing as interaction safety is not la-la land. It does not require forgetting about organizational goals or creating a "feel-good" environment. It is not about doing away with conflict, disagreement, or challenge. It is not about coddling people or accepting poor performance—rather, it is *raising the bar* on everyone and reaching the higher level of interaction needed for greater performance.

For over four decades, we have been fortunate to work with good organizations that want to be better. We have experienced the power of inclusion breakthroughs to create workplaces where people are unleashed and enabled to grow and become their biggest selves, to see their colleagues and partners as big, and to create teams in which each person and the team are bigger together and soar.

Our work has enabled organizations to develop more productive, effective, inclusive work environments by focusing on the most critical factor affecting performance: **interactions between people.**

Our last book, *Opening Doors to Teamwork and Collaboration*, described 4 Keys for enhancing those interactions:

- ▶ *Lean into Discomfort:* Encourage yourself and others to speak up and be BIG.

- ▶ *Listen as an Ally:* Work to understand and build on others' ideas instead of judging them.

- ▶ *State Your Intent and Intensity:* Let people know how committed you are to your ideas and what you need from them.

- ▶ *Share Your Street Corners:* Actively seek out others' perspectives to see all sides of the situation.

This book is about creating an environment in which people feel *safe enough* to apply those critical behaviors.

We have seen firsthand the power and effectiveness of the 4 Keys for improving interactions between individuals and teams. We have watched organizations blossom before our eyes as people have applied those behaviors and moved away from judging behaviors and toward joining interactions.

Using the 4 Keys has resulted in optimized interactions across levels, divisions, disciplines, and identity groups, as well as measurable improvements in productivity, quality, customer service, staff satisfaction, and bottom-line performance.

Time and again, people have told us about the positive changes they were leading and witnessing, expressing relief that their initial fears that the intervention was just another "flavor of the month" were unfounded. They were thrilled to have finally found a sustainable path for continuous improvement.

What accelerates this process—the foundation of these breakthroughs and behaviors—is the ability to create an environment of *interaction safety.*

Interaction safety is critical to the ability to join, connect, collaborate, innovate, and do our best work. It enables us to soar higher than any one of us could alone and to achieve more together than any of us could individually.

Organizations need *everyone's* best thinking, but few create environments to enable that. All too often, people hold back, testing whether their managers and team members will encourage them, listen to their ideas, and value their contributions—and, too often, people are failing the test.

Many organizations talk about the need for engagement and for people to stand up and speak out, but the trust needed for that level of interaction is often broken or missing.

This book provides the building blocks for creating a culture of interaction safety—the safety to soar. It is written for anyone who wants to contribute, from the shop floor to the C-suite. It is for *every* member of the organization—all have a role to play in creating interaction safety for themselves and their team members.

Our goal is to give you a clear path for making every one-on-one interaction, every group and team meeting, and your entire organization safe enough for people to engage fully and be willing and able to work collectively to address and solve the problems of today and the challenges of the future.

In this book, we focus on what the organization, its leaders, and every individual needs to do to create the environment and momentum that will produce a culture of interaction safety.

Interaction safety is a developmental process that consists of four levels. For each level, we identify common barriers to interaction safety and offer suggestions for how to move to the next level.

We hope organizations and their members aspire to achieve Level Four, in which interaction safety is a Way of Life. At Level Four, the organization's values, expectations, leadership practices, and human resource policies all align to create and support an environment of interaction safety

> where people are unleashed, where they don't hesitate to take risks, identify problems, join others in common purpose, and bring their best and boldest thinking.

How quickly an organization can achieve Level Four will depend on how much time, energy, and support its leaders and members are willing to commit. No one creates interaction safety alone. This is a journey in which people need to let go of some old mind-sets and be willing to co-create a new environment.

We hope the tools and insights in this book enable you and your colleagues to create the kind of workplace that will accelerate the trust, inclusion, and collaboration that are so vital to individual and collective success. Are you ready to start creating interaction safety?

It's time to make your organization safe enough to soar!

Fred and Judith

Let's Get Started

Introduction

Do You Feel Safe Enough to Soar?

Do you feel safe enough to

stand up and speak out at work?

be your best self so you can do your best work?

report a problem with a product or a process? How about with a colleague, team leader, or senior leader?

offer your best ideas? How about ideas you have that are *still in formation* but could possibly grow into breakthrough products or processes if shared, tweaked, and nurtured by a collaborative group of colleagues?

If you're a leader, you probably feel responsible for the physical safety of the people who report to you. Do you also accept responsibility for creating an environment in which people feel safe enough to *interact* freely and share their best ideas?

Do all the members of your team feel safe enough to report problems? To have honest conversations? To embrace different points of view? To do their best work?

Are you sure?

What are the costs of

▸ ideas not shared?

▸ questions not asked?

▸ issues not reported?

▸ solutions not offered?

▸ problems that remain unsolved?

▸ conflicts that fester and go unresolved?

Many organizations don't pay much attention to interaction safety. The default assumption is often, "I feel safe here, so I'm sure others do, too," or that it's each person's responsibility to either tough it out or fend for themselves.

When interaction safety is absent, people act small. They avoid interactions with anyone they are not completely comfortable with. They don't share their opinions. They don't share their ideas. They don't share information. They avoid taking the risks needed to move a conversation, an idea, or the organization forward.

When I don't feel safe . . .

. . . I know you are not getting the best out of me.

. . . I walk on eggshells and I'm careful about what I say.

. . . I fear being judged or made small.

. . . it is harder to join, to trust, and to accept different and new ideas or people.

Many organizations are now recognizing the need to create inclusive workplaces that leverage differences, invite all members to contribute their full range of skills and talents, and enable them to do their best work.

But . . . we still see many examples of organizations in which interaction safety (and even physical safety) does *not* exist. There are many organizations in which bullying, verbal abuse, and harassment (verbal or physical) are tolerated.

These are easily observable manifestations of unsafe environments. However, most of the behaviors, actions, and attitudes that create unsafe interactions are far more subtle.

Many organizations have a *long way to go* to achieve interaction safety.

What Is Interaction Safety?

Organizations are only as productive as the interactions that take place among people. Interaction safety encourages reasonable risk taking and inspires every individual to be brave enough to reach for higher goals and more ambitious possibilities.

It is an environment that makes people feel safe enough to share not just their best ideas but also their *still-in-formation* ideas.

It is a safety that accelerates building the trust so vital for inclusion and collaboration in one-on-one interactions, among teams, across departments, and throughout an organization.

When interaction safety exists, people know they will not be penalized, ostracized, demoted, made small, discounted, or shunned because of their thoughts, contributions, and conversations.

When interaction safety exists, the following default assumptions are made:

▶ We're all on the same team and the same side.

▶ All team members have the intention and the competence to add value.

▶ The best solutions are those that consider all angles and incorporate all relevant perspectives.

▶ The best route to success is building on one another's ideas rather than tearing them down.

▶ We can achieve more together than we can alone.

What It Feels Like

People trust that they are among allies. They feel able to give their best efforts, and they expect the same level of effort from their colleagues.

People feel encouraged to share their ideas without feeling judged or at risk. People are willing to consider viewpoints different from their own, to update their beliefs, and to admit what they don't know and ask for more information. People are comfortable addressing misunderstandings and disagreements.

People understand that we all have blind spots and we need to partner with others to get a complete view.

There's a sense of freedom: freedom to engage, learn, experiment, be wrong once in a while, try new things, and venture down untrodden paths.

There's more energy shared and less energy wasted. People invest their effort in generating, exploring, and developing new ideas rather than worrying about whether it is safe enough to share those ideas. The workplace energizes the workgroup, and the workgroup energizes its members.

What It Looks Like

People are honest and open with each other. They listen to each other respectfully and work to clarify and understand each other's points of view, seeking to add value rather than undercut one another. The norm is "Yes, and . . . ," not "Yes, but . . ." Conflicts are addressed directly and quickly.

Information flows quickly, problems are identified before they grow into crises, and new ideas are generated by ever-changing combinations of perspectives, skill sets, and disciplines.

People with different perspectives share and integrate their points of view rather than arguing about which is correct or more valuable. They offer challenging ideas and feedback, confident that everyone is committed to achieving the best outcome. People with different skills work together to solve problems better than they could have individually.

As more ideas are shared,

✓ people grow

✓ teams grow

✓ organizations grow.

There is greater speed to market, efficiency in process, improvement in quality, and retention of talent.

Four Levels of Interaction Safety

Level One: On Your Own

There is *no focus* on interaction safety in the workplace. The organization is characterized by behaviors that range from bullying to verbal or physical harassment and abuse to less overt actions such as sarcasm, shaming, and put-downs.

✓ When incidents that violate interaction safety occur, the organization sees them as one-off occurrences and they are usually blamed on a "bad apple."

✓ People are on their own, expected to fend for themselves, and often pitted against each other.

- ✓ People often feel judged and that they must constantly prove themselves without the benefit of the doubt.
- ✓ Individuals who report incidents may be labeled as "troublemakers" or "too sensitive."
- ✓ There are few, if any, human resources policies that address interaction safety.
- ✓ Leaders aren't concerned with making the workplace safe for interactions.

Level Two: Lip Service

There is *some focus* on interaction safety. The organization begins to recognize the importance of interaction safety, or at least the *appearance* of it, but does little to make interaction safety a cultural reality.

- ✓ When incidents that violate interaction safety occur, they are addressed as a human resources issue, but with no focus on the root cause.
- ✓ People experience a disconnect between the espoused values and actual behaviors of the organization and its leaders.
- ✓ People have little opportunity to learn skills for greater interaction safety.
- ✓ There may be human resources policies that address interaction safety, but they are unevenly enforced and focus more on disciplinary action than on addressing the root cause.
- ✓ Interaction safety is not directly connected to business outcomes.

Level Three: Islands of Safety

There is a *great deal of focus* on interaction safety. The organization is actively working to make interaction safety a cultural reality, but the practices that support it are not consistent throughout the organization. Level Three organizations recognize that it is a journey to create this new environment.

✓ When incidents that violate interaction safety occur, the organization addresses them swiftly and takes action regarding the root cause.

✓ The organization strives to provide the tools needed for interaction safety.

✓ Individuals feel safe enough to soar within their teams or in a specific workgroup, but not everywhere.

✓ While many senior leaders see interaction safety as foundational to higher performance, some worry that the change threatens the organization's formula for success.

Level Four: Way of Life

In Level Four organizations, interaction safety is the *Way of Life* and understood as a critical factor for overall success. There is an organization-wide environment in which people are safe enough to soar and individuals, teams, and the organization reap the benefits of productivity, collaboration, innovation, and people doing their best work individually and collectively.

✓ When incidents that violate interaction safety occur, they are seen as outside the norm and as individual and organizational failures needing immediate attention.

- ✓ People feel free to bring their best selves to the workplace—to contribute, grow, and partner without reservation.

- ✓ Everyone is seen as having value to contribute.

- ✓ Efforts are focused on how to sustain and constantly improve the culture, and team members are aware that it takes vigilance and constant work to maintain and continuously improve the quality of performance and interaction safety.

- ✓ Leaders see interaction safety as connected to the work of the organization and the achievement of higher performance.

- ✓ The organization regularly assesses interaction safety for continuous improvement.

Moving to Level Four

To move from your organization's current level to Level Four will require conscious leadership and advocacy at all levels of the organization, but no movement will happen without dissatisfaction with the current environment. Our model of change entails the following process:

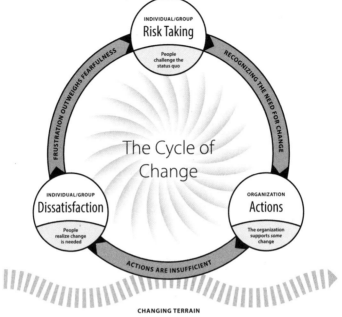

Individual and Group Dissatisfaction

The process of moving from one level of interaction safety to the next begins when individuals or leaders become dissatisfied with the current environment. They see the costs to individuals and the organization of continuing down the current path without change. Individuals can't do their best work. There is loss of key talent. The company underperforms. Employee surveys indicate a gap between the organization's values and behaviors. There is growing turnover and an increase in incident reports. Dissatisfaction grows as people know they and the organization could do better.

The more widely held the dissatisfaction with what is or is not happening, the greater the pressure for change.

Individual and Group Risk Taking

Once individuals or leaders are willing to acknowledge there is a level of dissatisfaction, *someone needs to take a risk* to stand up and speak out about the lack of interaction safety and its impact on individual and organizational performance. Speaking up can be particularly risky if the organization is at Level One or Two, where interaction safety is not a part of expectations for how individuals and teams work with one another. No matter where an organization is, it takes courage for people to speak up and question the status quo.

Organization Actions

Once the issues are raised, leaders have a choice to ignore or minimize those issues or take action for greater interaction safety. Leaders need to acknowledge the dissatisfaction, establish new expectations, and implement actions to move to the next level. Without action, risk taking will be reduced and dissatisfaction increased.

The Cycle of Change

The cycle of change is iterative. When the organization has taken actions to move to the next level, at some point, there will be dissatisfaction with the new state because people's expectations are raised, and the cycle begins again.

Even when an organization reaches Level Four, because the environmental context is always changing, the organization will need to continue to take steps to sustain and improve interaction safety.

Where Is Your Organization?

We have seen and worked with individuals and teams that run the gamut of levels. Some parts of an organization are often well behind or well ahead of others. Many would like to believe they are further ahead than they are.

Even in organizations that are mostly at Level One or Two, people have experienced settings where interaction safety enables people to contribute freely, where people are excited to come to work and do great things together every day, where there is a "we" mindset that permeates their team.

You may think your organization is safe. But is it safe enough that people can fully bring their ideas and experiences to the workplace?

Is It Safe Enough to Soar?

The next sections describe the characteristics of the work environment at each level, illustrated with short scenarios so you can diagnose your organization, plus tips for identifying and mobilizing dissatisfaction to propel your organization to the next level.

As you read the scenarios, you might reflect on the following:

▶ Have you experienced, seen, or heard of a similar situation in your organization in the past year?

▶ How have you and others responded?

▶ What actions have you taken to create greater interaction safety to support the individual or situation?

On to Level One

Level One
On Your Own

Let's start at Level One:
On Your Own

In a Level One organization, there is no awareness of the importance of safe interactions in the workplace. There is no understanding that the quality of people's interactions with one another might affect the quality of their work experience or their effort, output, and ability to collaborate with one another.

At Level One, there is *no focus* on interaction safety. People are expected to fend for themselves.

In other words, **you're on your own.**

Let's explore how people interact at Level One. Compare what happens here with what happens in your workplace. If these things seem normal to you, it is likely that you work in a Level One workplace.

In a Level One workplace, people compete to show their merit and worth. Until they pay their dues and establish themselves in the organizational pecking order, they must constantly prove themselves. New ideas and new people are scrutinized with suspicion.

New people are often ignored, hazed, harassed, or bullied. "Incidents" are ignored, explained away as misunderstandings, or blamed on the newcomer who "hasn't learned the ropes."

At Level One, you keep your head down and learn your place.

People judge one another constantly. Some people put down other people's ideas so they can advance their own. Many others keep their ideas to themselves to avoid criticism. Conversations include sarcasm, put-downs, criticism, mean jokes, and subtle and not-so-subtle digs.

It helps to have thick skin.

You are expected to give as good as you get. If you can't, you learn to shut up, keep your head down, and stay out of the way.

If you make a mistake or even a minor slipup, you are judged and not given the benefit of the doubt. You might be dressed down publicly in meetings or email chains.

If you get labeled, the label is likely to stick for a long, long time because people have long memories. Many find it's easier to just keep their ideas to themselves to avoid criticism.

People who complain about the environment are identified as "whiners." Whiners are easy targets for increased bullying. They either learn to keep their problems to themselves or leave.

People walk on eggshells.

It's safer to be small and not stick out.

Safety beyond the physical, life-threatening sense is ignored at all levels: individual, group, and organizational. When the organization signals that raising issues about problems with products or processes—the actual work being done—isn't okay, people quickly realize that voicing their own feelings regarding interaction safety is dangerous.

We know better than to be the bearers of bad news because they *shoot the messengers.*

Speaking up about interaction safety issues regarding team members and managers is taboo. Raising organizational problems of any kind happens mostly in exit interviews . . . or is likely to lead to one.

There is no awareness of the barriers people face that prevent them from expressing their ideas or doing their best work. It is simply not in the organization's Way of Life.

Leaders see and describe any discussion of interaction safety as "soft stuff" and see it as a waste of time. There is a belief that people should just get on with the work at hand.

Now, let me introduce you to Harry, who has worked in his organization for years.

Harry is fed up. He's decided it's time to talk to his manager. He has come to expect sarcastic remarks in meetings, but after years of putting up with it, he finds his confidence eroding. It isn't spoken about much, but he can tell that more and more of his colleagues feel the same way. The last time one of Harry's colleagues spoke up, he got slammed for it. The same has repeatedly happened to others.

Harry has decided he can no longer tolerate this. He knows he has some great ideas to share, but the effort it takes to get a new idea discussed and the reaction he receives are sapping his energy. He feels many of the meetings he participates in are a waste of time. People are not sharing their thoughts because it is just not safe enough. Generally, people only discuss real issues in the "meeting before the meeting" (or after)—not with managers or others they don't know well, but privately with team members they can trust.

Harry decides to raise his concerns with his manager, with whom he has a good relationship. When he does, his manager responds with appreciation that Harry has shared his concerns, but then he adds, "C'mon Harry, you know how it is around here. Don't take it personally. That's just the way it is."

Harry realizes what his manager has said is true. He decides he is just going to do his job and keep his head down . . . just like the rest of his colleagues.

At Level One, these kinds of interactions seem normal.

Are they "normal" in your organization?

- People are afraid to speak up.
- When it comes to interacting with leaders, people only speak when spoken to.
- Minefields are everywhere, so you tread carefully.
- If you make a mistake, it is remembered and could be career limiting, even if it is small.
- People have to look out for themselves.
- New people must be quiet and wait their turn.
- When good performers leave, the organization says negative things about them to justify their leaving.
- There are lots of unwritten rules. If you haven't been around long enough to know them, it is safest to keep your mouth shut.
- Leaders are not comfortable with people pushing back or bringing their own thinking to the table.
- Jokes, ridicule, and even hazing are common.
- People don't give each other the benefit of the doubt—you have to prove yourself continually.
- If you complain about someone being disrespectful, you are coached to tough it out and ignore statements that might be demeaning.
- If a particular leader seems to punish, bully, or judge team members, people will say, "That's just

the way she/he is," or position it as a virtue. The leader is "demanding" or "has high standards." They might suggest you transfer out of that leader's area as others have done.

- ▶ In meetings, people commonly punch holes in each other's ideas.

- ▶ Even when people agree, the agreement starts with, "Yes, but . . ."

- ▶ People are rewarded more for criticism than for critical thinking.

- ▶ People compete to demonstrate that they are the smartest in the room.

- ▶ People walk on eggshells. They worry that any mistake they make will be long remembered.

- ▶ People who report incidents are as likely to be blamed for them as the parties they lodge complaints against. All parties involved may be warned about the consequences if the behavior happens again.

In a Level One organization, new ideas and new people are not often welcomed . . .

. . . as Pat, a new hire, is learning.

A new hire, Pat, is a highly prized recruit. The company's hiring staff spent months searching for, recruiting, vetting, and finally hiring Pat. They believe she will bring fresh perspectives and expertise the company sorely needs. The company hopes, based on her track record and their interactions with her, that Pat can make an immediate impact in their sales and customer satisfaction.

In her first weeks on the job, Pat feels her new colleagues are being polite but cautious. She can tell they are keeping her at arm's length. When she makes a suggestion, her colleagues point out all sorts of flaws in it. They make comments like, "You don't understand the situation here yet," and, "We tried something like that before and it didn't work," and, "That's not the way we do things around here."

Some of her more sympathetic teammates take her aside and coach her to slow down, relax, and "learn how we do things here."

Pat had been warned that joining the organization could be tough, and she came into the job with her eyes open, excited about this new opportunity, and certain she was strong enough to handle it. She had been in other organizations that were "sink or swim" but was always successful in those environments.

Although Pat was expecting some of this, she is finding herself exhausted each day when she leaves work. Before long, she stops bringing in her new ideas. After six months at the company, Pat is thinking it might be time to update her resume once again. She thinks that if she left, no one would really care.

How We Interact in Meetings: Level One

"Normal" behaviors, interactions, and responses

Written rules and road signs	There are no statements about the importance of interaction safety.
When someone is talking	Keep your head down. Wait your turn to talk. Or judge and poke holes in what the person has said.
Interactions with the meeting leader	It is the leader's meeting. Only speak when spoken to.
Interactions with other team members	Only interact with other team members when absolutely necessary. Protect yourself and your team from being belittled.
When someone challenges an idea	Go on the attack or avoid interaction.
Outcome of interactions	Interactions are passive-aggressive. Time and energy are wasted. There is no trust, inclusion, or collaboration.

Leaders in Level One organizations are often thought of as "bosses."

Mary, a senior vice president, is Tony's boss.

Mary's team is working on a critical project. The team has been making good progress, but today Tony sent Mary and the other team members an email about a major problem that will delay the project by at least three weeks.

Mary is furious. She fires off an email to Tony—copying the rest of the team—telling him this is unacceptable. Her email starts off, "How could someone with your knowledge let this happen?" The rest of her reply expresses her opinion of Tony's ineptitude in not foreseeing the problem. After sending the email, Mary feels better for having made her point. She is sure it will keep Tony and the team on their toes.

Tony and the team members have become numb to such outbursts from Mary. This latest outburst reminds them of why they spend so much time working around Mary and hiding problems from her whenever possible.

People who don't fit the organization's traditional profile are few and far between.

Akasha often hears she is "different" from how others expected her to be.

Akasha realizes that hardly anyone in the company is treated with respect. At first, she felt she was being treated more harshly because she was one of the few women of color. Now, she sees that many, if not most, people in the company are treated disrespectfully. This realization was somehow almost comforting.

She is aware of the fine line she must walk to be successful. In a recent meeting, Pablo, a facilitator, was called Pancho, which she knew was intended as a derogatory remark. Akasha often hears people in meetings telling jokes about others not in the room. Sometimes she hears colleagues using offensive terms to refer to others. She doesn't join in, but she feels as if she is colluding by staying silent and watching other people in the room laugh.

She recently heard that a senior leader made a homophobic remark at an offsite meeting, and another leader, in front of others, "jokingly" threatened to hit a team member with a bat . . . and neither leader's behavior was addressed or even criticized.

Akasha has been told she has a bright future with the company. She works hard to demonstrate her competence every day in order to fit in and make others feel comfortable around her. Yet there are many moments when she feels alone, with few people to talk to about how her differences and experiences affect her daily life in the organization. She is noticing that not only is she withdrawing personally but she is also more hesitant to voice her ideas.

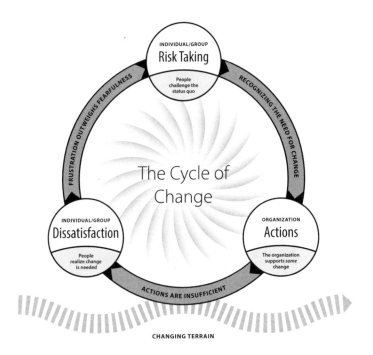

INDIVIDUAL/GROUP
Risk Taking

People challenge the status quo

RECOGNIZING THE NEED FOR CHANGE

FRUSTRATION OUTWEIGHS FEARFULNESS

The Cycle of Change

INDIVIDUAL/GROUP
Dissatisfaction

People realize change is needed

ORGANIZATION
Actions

The organization supports *some* change

ACTIONS ARE INSUFFICIENT

CHANGING TERRAIN

Moving to the Next Level

Roots of Dissatisfaction

Here are some of the signs of dissatisfaction at Level One.

▶ There is fear of retribution for challenging the status quo.

▶ A high value is placed on conformity and loyalty to current cultural norms.

- There is an assumption that leaders know best.

- An "us versus them" mind-set is prevalent.

- Any difference is seen as a threat.

- People are punished—put down verbally, sidelined for development opportunities, labeled as troublemakers—if they step outside the current norms. They must fit in.

- People feel judged.

- People who raise a problem get labeled as *the* problem.

- In meetings, people have to remain silent and watch as their colleagues are made small or outright attacked.

So, what can *you* do to move to Level Two?

Individual Actions: Taking Risks

☑ Be willing to let at least one other person know that you are feeling bullied or diminished.

☑ Engage team members and others you trust about how to create safer interactions.

☑ End the collusion of silence: Don't laugh at jokes that put others down. Support others when they are not being treated with respect and are made small (for example, through sarcasm or bullying behavior), even if that support has to be given privately.

☑ Identify and share what you need to feel safe (for example, letting people know how they can support you or asking someone to have your back when you are not present).

☑ When an email chain includes name-calling, don't engage. If you are directly involved, pick up the phone and talk to the individual.

Leaders:

Here are some things you can do to make interactions safer for your team members.

Leader and Organization Actions

☑ Stop accepting an unsafe environment as "normal" or just the way things are.

☑ Let team members know you will not accept sarcasm, put-downs, or judging behavior within your team.

- ☑ Identify and eliminate your behaviors that may be experienced by others as put-downs.
- ☑ Establish organizational anti-harassment policies.
- ☑ Provide protection for whistle-blowers.
- ☑ Track incidents and complaints.

On to Level Two

Level Two
Lip Service

The organization and its leaders have begun to pay *lip service* **to interaction safety.**

At Level Two, things start to change a bit.

There is *some focus* on interaction safety. Some people *talk* about it!

At Level Two, the organization begins to take the first steps toward interaction safety. The organization has begun to make public statements about the importance of interaction safety in the workplace, but it has not done much to make it happen.

The organization may have interaction-safety-oriented words that it uses. It might have added interaction safety to its values statement, its recruiting materials, its corporate communications, and even its meeting-room signage.

At Level Two, the organization begins to recognize the importance of interaction safety, or at least the *appearance* of interaction safety. But a Level Two organization has done little to make interaction safety *a reality*. The organization has yet to discover the connection between greater interaction safety and tangible bottom-line results. There is a disconnect between the organization's stated values and its actual behaviors; they are misaligned.

In Level Two organizations, leaders begin to pay attention to distress signals in the workplace environment and in employee surveys. Leaders begin to note inequities in treatment, discouragement and dissatisfaction, and plans for departure. When reviewed in concert with other data, such as employee turnover rates, sick time, annual performance reviews, and incident reports, it becomes clear to some leaders that a level of pain exists in the organization. Before they begin to see any potential benefit from interaction safety, organizational leaders first see the cost of its absence.

I don't know whether this interaction safety stuff will do us any good, but I'm pretty sure the lack of it is costing us a lot.

Faced with reports of embarrassing or costly incidents, customer-service complaints, or issues with quality control and productivity, some leaders in the organization begin to discuss the importance of creating a safer environment. This encourages people to be more willing to contribute their best efforts and best thinking and to speak up to identify problems and possible solutions.

Leaders give speeches, champion the cause in town hall meetings, and issue edicts declaring the organization's commitment to a safer workplace for voicing opinions.

And it *does* make a difference! People become a bit more willing to speak up about the need for interaction safety and to report serious incidents of harassment, intimidation, bias, and disrespectful behavior.

The overall number of unsafe interactions may even decrease.

At the end of the day, the speeches, edicts, and leadership advocacy don't go far enough and may feel like lip service to some. There is more willingness to address blatant incidents on an individual basis, but some leaders and middle managers who create an unsafe environment still get promoted because they achieve business results.

Reporting an incident of harassment or other unsafe interaction might not be a career-limiting move, but perpetrating such actions still isn't either. Many incidents are still overlooked or excused. People who have had their hopes raised by the words of the organization's leaders end up frustrated by the lack of substantive, consistent action. And while people may indeed feel less unsafe, little is done to ensure that the organization is safer for interactions.

 Interaction safety rules and training are more about compliance than improving the quality of people's work experience and interactions.

Leaders support the espoused value of creating a safe culture but do not have the skills or incentive to act differently. Actions reflect a need to comply with workplace safety regulations (for example, addressing harassment and bullying) more than a real commitment to creating a different kind of interaction in the workplace.

Although increased awareness of interaction safety issues enables people to talk more openly about feeling unsafe, the number of complaints about the lack of safety may increase because people are beginning to feel safer to speak up.

There is also likely to be a fairly widespread sense of loss for the "good old days" when people didn't complain about insensitive jokes, insults, ideas they did not like, judgmental behavior, or the use of racist, sexist, or homophobic language. People will complain about the need to be "politically correct." They may use appropriate language but in a sarcastic way in order to diminish it.

Like Ethan, many people are hoping for change but are not sure the organization is ready for it.

Ethan has just seen the results from the latest employee survey. He and many of his colleagues were pleased that the organization asked team members how they experienced the work environment.

Ethan went out on a limb and honestly identified ways in which the organization was not safe for people to speak up. He is encouraged when he hears leaders make statements about the importance of the survey results. The senior team pledged to create a work environment in which people are engaged and speak up.

However, he is disheartened when one of the worst offenders in leadership is promoted. And then one of his colleagues is called into her manager's office and asked about her responses on the survey, even though they had been told it was anonymous.

Ethan wonders: Is this just another program of the month, or can we realistically hope that things will actually change?

There is growing awareness of the need for interaction safety, but little action.

It is mostly just talk.

At Level Two, *these* kinds of interactions seem normal.

Are they "normal" in your organization?

▶ Some leaders say the right words about the need for interaction safety but don't consistently demonstrate the behaviors that would create it. It is not a cultural norm.

▶ People are confused by mixed messages about whether interaction safety is really valued.

▶ Leaders and team members are not comfortable with people pushing back or bringing their own thinking to the table. Leaders and colleagues question their loyalty, treat them coldly, and label them as troublemakers.

▶ Individuals whose actions or inactions perpetuate an unsafe environment continue to be promoted to leadership positions.

▶ Some leaders who actively work to create interaction safety are teased or derided ("You're getting soft" or "You're losing your edge") by other leaders.

▶ There are no formal or informal rewards for individuals and leaders who are creating a safer environment for interactions.

Leaders say they want team members to speak up, but Sing Ping wonders if they really mean something else.

Sing Ping joined the company because of the values of teamwork and collaboration that she heard about in the interview process. She was encouraged by the company's stated commitment to creating an environment in which people can speak up. Walking around the building during the interview, she saw signs in conference rooms and hallways about the importance of listening and creating trust and the need for collaboration.

At today's meeting, Sing Ping plans to make a suggestion she has been thinking about for several weeks but to which she has been unsure how others might respond.

Finally, her turn comes, and she starts to present her suggestion. Before she even gets half of it out of her mouth, one of the other people in the meeting starts telling her what is wrong with what she has said so far. Others quickly pile on. Sing Ping tries to share her complete idea, but the team is too busy talking over her to listen. After a while her manager says, "Thanks, Sing Ping," in a dismissive manner, and the meeting moves on to another topic. She thinks, "So much for our commitment to listening and being open to new ideas."

How We Interact in Meetings: Level Two

"Normal" behaviors, interactions, and responses

Written rules and road signs	Signs about interaction safety are posted but not followed.
When someone is talking	People listen when it is something that directly relates to them. Mostly, people just wait for the pause that means it's their turn to speak.
Interactions with the meeting leader	Comment (guardedly) when you have something important to say.
Interactions with other team members	State agreements in meetings. State disagreements privately with those you feel safe with.
When someone challenges an idea	Calculate the risk of responding. Talk to others rather than directly to the individual.
Outcome of interactions	Performance is suboptimal, problems are not fully explored, and all points of view do not come forward. There is little trust, inclusion, or collaboration.

Signs on the meeting room walls encourage people to speak up and share their best ideas.

But for Jill, Akiema, and others, there's an unwritten qualifier: ". . . but not too much."

Jill and Akiema have the same manager, but he doesn't treat them the same. Jill experiences her manager, George, as respectful and engaging, so she can't understand why Akiema, who is a woman of color, sees and experiences the organization so differently.

Jill enjoys a good working relationship with George, and the two frequently go to lunch together. Akiema experiences George as judging and repeatedly criticizing her work, even though others she works with see her as a high performer. She is afraid to bring this up to George. As a woman of color, Akiema has to tread carefully to avoid the stereotypical "angry black woman" label. She knows that no matter how careful she is, any issue she raises might cause people to see her that way. Although she keeps hearing the organization say it wants people to speak up, she does not feel safe enough to do so.

When Akiema shares her concern with Jill, Jill cautions her not to raise the issue. Jill agrees that, although they are hearing more about creating safety, for the most part there is little action. Jill doesn't believe things have changed all that much. In fact, just last week, George complained about someone who had challenged him. Jill agrees with Akiema's concerns and sees how Akiema could experience their manager in the way she described. After the conversation, Akiema decides she is going to continue to work as hard as she has been and position herself to transfer out if things do not change.

Trying to build interaction safety can feel awkward at first, as Martin is learning. But he *is* learning.

Martin wants to be a better leader, and he's working at it. He's glad the company is supporting him to become more of the leader he wants to be. He has taken several training courses to learn new skills for better employee engagement, active listening, and the creation of a safer environment for interactions.

He knows he isn't perfect, and at times he still slips into old behaviors. He remembers the meeting he was in last week in which he talked over and interrupted Sheila. He immediately regretted it, knowing Sheila must have experienced it as demeaning. Martin apologized after the meeting, but the damage was done.

Martin is hoping Sheila and others will give him the benefit of the doubt and some grace rather than judge him when his behaviors may not be aligned with how he says he wants to interact. He hopes the team understands that he is still learning and that he needs everyone's help in creating this new environment.

Martin wonders if he should have made the apology to Sheila publicly instead of privately, so everyone could see he is trying. But he also worries that some team members may be holding on to the past and might not have heard his apology as sincere. Martin knows he needs to change in order to create a different environment. But will the team members be willing to trust and let go of the past?

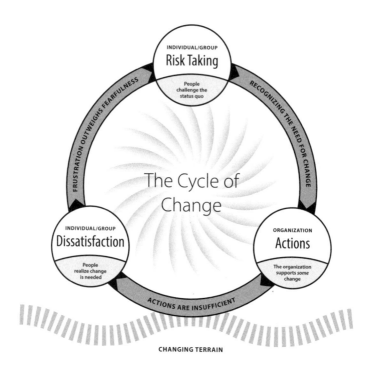

Moving to the Next Level

Roots of Dissatisfaction

Here are some of the signs of dissatisfaction at Level Two.

- ► The status quo is valued; change is perceived as a threat to organizational stability.

- ► Signs stating the need for interaction safety are posted on the walls of the meeting rooms but are not followed.

- There is no linkage between how people interact with one another and organizational performance. Interaction safety is seen as "soft stuff."

- There is an assumption that people are easily replaced.

- People are incentivized to achieve business goals, without regard for how those outcomes are achieved.

- There are few, if any, role models for or successful examples of creating interaction safety.

- There is a lack of clarity about what interaction safety really means, and this results in people being too fearful or "too nice" to have honest conversations and give direct feedback and coaching.

- When interaction safety training does take place, there is little or no transfer of learnings to the workplace and day-to-day interactions. Many treat training as a check-the-box activity.

OK, let's see . . .

What will it take to move to Level Three?

Individual Actions: Taking Risks

☑ Publicly identify and acknowledge team members and leaders who are working to make interaction safety part of the way they operate. Provide support and energy to them for their actions.

- [✓] Let people know you are committed to practicing interaction safety. Invite them to give you feedback when they experience you creating a safe environment, as well as when you are not.

- [✓] Be an ally for colleagues who feel unsafe. Speak up in meetings, let them know you see the behavior, and give them public support.

- [✓] Identify how interaction safety is making an impact on achieving results.

Leaders:

Here are some things you can do to make interactions safer for your team members.

Leader and Organization Actions

- [✓] Let others know how you are working to create a safer environment for interaction.

- [✓] Be willing to be visible and vulnerable in your learning and behavior.

- [✓] Listen to people's concerns, whether expressed in surveys, complaints, or discussions. Let them know how you are working to address their concerns.

- [✓] Work with your peers to make interaction safety more than "lip service."

- [✓] Connect the importance of interaction safety to performance.

- [✓] Engage others at all levels in discussions about how to create a safer environment for interactions.

Act on what you learn and demonstrate you are listening.

- [✓] Look for and call out examples of individuals and teams that are demonstrating interaction safety. Highlight the behaviors people are demonstrating and also highlight the positive impact on the organization's performance.

- [✓] Include in promotion criteria leaders' ability to model and create interaction safety in their teams.

- [✓] Conduct education on interaction safety and hold people accountable for demonstrating behaviors.

On to Level Three

Level Three
Islands of Safety

What you'll find at Level Three:

Islands of Safety

At Level Three,
the organization moves
from *lip service* to *action*.

(But it doesn't happen
everywhere.)

At Level Three, the organization aggressively works to create interaction safety. The organization and its leaders not only express the need for creating an environment in which honest, productive, and collaborative interactions occur; they take substantive actions to make it a reality. Interaction safety is recognized as foundational for a culture of inclusion and a path to higher performance for individuals, teams, and the organization.

But not everyone is on board with the effort. Many, including some of the leaders, still see interaction safety as primarily a human resources issue and not connected to the organization's business outcomes or bottom-line interests.

As a whole, the organization's new policies and actions are moving in the direction of greater interaction safety. However, the actions are not implemented throughout the organization. There are islands where interaction safety has become the standard way of operating, but there are other parts of the organization where the old "look out for yourself" culture still holds.

In some workgroups, interaction safety is seen as a route to better collaboration and more productive teams and partnerships.

But in others, it is still seen as "soft" and nonessential or as just another program of the month.

Some work teams quickly embrace the premise and practice of interaction safety, and their members thrive, both individually and collectively.

Some find it difficult to extend trust beyond the boundaries of their own tight circle of familiarity, or even within it. Others hold back. Some even *hope* that the effort fails so that they can soon return to the way things were.

And others look around and say to themselves, "I want what they have," noticing that where there is more interaction safety, there is less turnover and better results.

The benefits of interaction safety immediately clicked with Willie's team.

But will it help them partner with a work team from another division? Willie is pleased with how quickly things are changing in the organization to make interaction safety a reality. He appreciates his team members and how they are working together.

When there are difficult issues, the team seems to rise to the occasion. Willie rarely finds himself censoring what he has to say, and other team members share their points of view freely and respectfully. They are a diverse team, and they often have honest conversations about their differences in background, experiences, and skill sets. They capitalize on those differences, especially when they are faced with complex problems or decisions.

However, Willie and his team have just been given a new task. They will need to work with a team from a different division, and he is not looking forward to it. The other team has a reputation for withholding data, being judgmental, and being unwilling to collaborate or address conflicts directly. They have not yet accepted the new way of interacting. When the two teams have worked together in the past, everything slowed down. People were frustrated by the lack of direct communication, the project suffered from the other team's lack of input, and often there was a lack of agreement on the best actions to take. Working with the other team resulted in the project taking longer and costing more.

Willie is struggling with whether he will be able to build trust and collaboration with the other team if they are holding very different images of success and how to interact to achieve that success.

Willie takes a deep breath and walks into the meeting, ready to engage in a positive way . . . and hoping the feeling is mutual. .

At Level Three, *these* kinds of interactions seem normal.

Are they "normal" in your organization?

► Some individuals treat all their colleagues as partners and allies, but others still start every interaction from a judging mind-set.

► Certain parts of the organization are seen as desirable places to work because they are islands of interaction safety.

► While some human resources and management systems are changing to create a safe environment for interactions, the organization's reward systems, policies, and practices are lagging behind the vision and are still not fully congruent with supporting interaction safety.

► Individuals who are sometimes abusive are dealt with swiftly—coached, disciplined, or removed— and it is generally understood that such behavior is not acceptable. But in some workgroups and divisions, people still get away with it.

► Most people trust their team members, but some individuals still hold back.

► Leaders recognize that many people may be holding on to the past. They work hard to earn and build trust in every interaction.

► Trust exists within the boundaries of a tight circle or workgroup.

For leaders, the job of creating interaction safety for others can start with trusting that its practice actually works.

Barbara knows leaders must learn to practice what they preach. Over the past few years, Barbara has seen many changes in how leaders are expected to interact with others. As a member of the senior leadership team, she feels confident about the team's ability to serve as role models for the new environment they are working so hard to create.

Barbara believes her peers are committed to this new way of working, so she is surprised and concerned when she witnesses an incident in a meeting in which Paul, another senior leader, acts in ways that are counter to the new norms. Specifically, he talks over a few people and is unnecessarily critical of one of the team members.

Given the commitment to lean into discomfort and address disagreements, she decides she can't let Paul's behavior go without comment. After the meeting, she asks him if they can talk and if he is open to feedback.

Paul says that he is, and when they sit down together, Barbara describes the behaviors she witnessed and how she experienced them. She asks Paul what was going on, since his behavior seemed inconsistent with what he has said publicly regarding his commitment to supporting interaction safety and to demonstrating behaviors that create that environment.

At first, Paul is taken aback by Barbara's comments. But as he thinks for a moment, he realizes he came into the meeting anxious about a personal matter and those feelings spilled over to the meeting. Paul thanks Barbara for her concern and for taking the time to talk with him honestly and in the spirit of interaction safety. He had not realized the toll the personal issue was having. They talk about how Paul can repair any damage he may have done with the people involved, and they agree to give each other feedback like this in the future.

Both Paul and Barbara agree that this conversation never would have happened before the organization began focusing on creating interaction safety. They see it as an example of being honest and authentic with each other and as a good model for how to collaborate for the greater good of the team and the organization.

We support each other and give each other the benefit of the doubt.

Well . . . many of us do, most of the time.

In an unsafe world, safety can't be assumed, so we need to take conscious steps to create it every day.

How We Interact in Meetings: Level Three

"Normal" behaviors, interactions, and responses

Written rules and road signs	Signs in the room promote interaction safety. Some individuals and teams refer to them a lot, others not at all.
When someone is talking	People test whether this is a group in which interaction safety is a norm and respond accordingly.
Interactions with the meeting leader	People hold an expectation that they have something to offer. Everyone expects to, and is expected to, contribute.
Interactions with other team members	Interactions are free, open, and supportive. People know the ideal is not yet a reality everywhere and so they are sometimes cautious.
When someone challenges an idea	The norm is to listen and try to see the other's point of view. Disrespectful challenges are rare and usually called out.
Outcome of interactions	Uneven levels of skill and commitment lead to uneven outcomes. There are islands of trust, inclusion, collaboration, and high performance.

New people are often appreciated for their fresh perspectives . . .

. . . but given the islands of interaction safety, sometimes they feel like Ping-Pong balls.

Daniel is new to the organization. He has been spending a lot of time and effort trying to figure out how he fits into the culture and how best to interact with others and contribute. While the organization has clearly made a lot of strides in its commitment to creating an environment of interaction safety, it still has some way to go.

At times, Daniel feels like a Ping-Pong ball. In one setting, he finds the team starts its meetings by reaffirming norms for interaction safety and sees members really living and demonstrating those norms. However, in other meetings, it seems that interaction safety is not on anyone's screen.

As he goes from meeting to meeting, he wonders: Which is the company's true culture?

For some, change is moving too fast, and for others, too slow.

The Diversity and Inclusion Council is at a crossroad. Celia has been a member of the Diversity and Inclusion Council for some time and has been pleased to see how the organization has progressed in creating an environment in which it is safer to speak up, particularly with respect to issues of diversity and inclusion. However, as the Council discusses this progress, some are not as positive or optimistic about where the organization is or the strides that have been made.

Roberto shares that he is still experiencing the "old culture" of jokes and biases. They are unquestioned in his part of the organization. As the Council discusses the current state, they agree things are progressing well in some parts of the organization but not in others. Chen asks, "How many years have we been doing this? We need to determine whether we really have the support of the organization. Are the leaders serious, or are we just wasting our time? We all have day jobs!"

Council members agree there is resistance. Many feel that progress is moving way too slow in creating a more inclusive and diverse environment in which interaction safety builds a culture of trust and collaboration. But they also acknowledge that the changes are being made too fast for others.

The Council agrees that it is time to re-engage the senior leaders to reaffirm their commitment, get everyone on board, and move the effort to the next level.

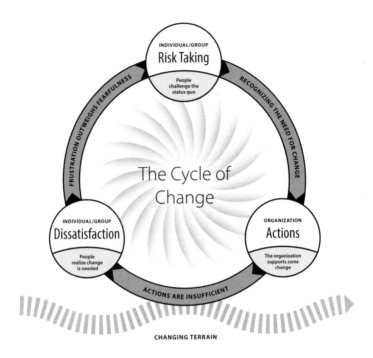

The Cycle of Change

INDIVIDUAL/GROUP
Risk Taking
People challenge the status quo

RECOGNIZING THE NEED FOR CHANGE

FRUSTRATION OUTWEIGHS FEARFULNESS

INDIVIDUAL/GROUP
Dissatisfaction
People realize change is needed

ORGANIZATION
Actions
The organization supports *some* change

ACTIONS ARE INSUFFICIENT

CHANGING TERRAIN

Moving to the Next Level

Roots of Dissatisfaction

Here are some of the signs of dissatisfaction at Level Three.

► Interaction safety is applied and practiced inconsistently.

► People still remember the past, and many don't fully trust their experience of interaction safety as sustainable.

- Interaction safety is not widely understood as critical to organizational success.

- The organization's reward systems, policies, and practices are lagging behind the vision and are still not fully congruent with supporting interaction safety.

- Some people assume that since they feel safe, others must as well. It can be hard for them to understand that the environment outside their bubble of safety might be different.

- Within teams, there are varying levels of interaction safety depending on the issue at hand—when timelines are tight and the pressure is on, they may revert to old behaviors.

- Islands are creating curiosity and a greater desire for interaction safety in other teams.

It's time to *soar*! Let's move to Level Four!

Individual Actions: Taking Risks

☑ Publicly hold yourself and others accountable for creating interaction safety in meetings and all interactions.

☑ Be an ally for interaction safety for new people and others who are learning the culture.

☑ Share what you are doing to create interaction safety and how it supports individual, team, and organizational effectiveness.

☑ Show support and appreciation when others act to create interaction safety.

☑ When you don't feel safe, be willing to lean into discomfort and let others know what you need to feel safe.

 Leaders:

Here are some things you can do to make interactions safer for your team members.

Leader and Organization Actions

☑ Work to make sure all human resources and management systems, policies, and practices fully support the creation of interaction safety, in both letter and spirit.

☑ Recognize that you and other leaders are learning and accept that there will be a learning curve. Actively engage to receive regular feedback on how (and what) you are doing, as individual leaders and as a group.

☑ Recognize that the history of the lack of interaction safety won't be undone quickly or easily. Actively work to build the necessary connections and relationships that build trust.

☑ Seek new ways to improve your ability to create and foster an environment of interaction safety.

☑ Talk to your team members about what they need for greater interaction safety and work to co-create that environment with your team members.

- ✓ Publicly praise team members who demonstrate behaviors that support interaction safety.

- ✓ Create recognition awards for interaction safety.

- ✓ In new-hire orientation and other training programs, include interaction safety as a key expectation for individual and organizational success.

- ✓ Track the impact of interaction safety on the achievement of organizational goals—for example, time to market, innovation, problem solving, and customer satisfaction.

On to Level Four

Level Four
Way of Life

At Level Four,
interaction safety is a
Way of Life.

Here, people feel *safe enough to soar*!

At Level Four, people feel free to voice their ideas. Not just their safest and best ideas, but also their brand-new ideas, whether half or fully baked . . .

Because their colleagues and leaders *listen* to them.

And *support* them.

And *build on* their ideas to create *better* ideas together that none could have imagined individually.

And all share in the credit. But more importantly, all share in the *joy* of creation and collaboration and being part of something greater than themselves.

We don't have to work together for years before giving each other the benefit of the doubt.

We *start* with an implicit assumption of trust.

At Level Four, interaction safety is foundational.

In a Level Four organization, every interaction begins with an implicit assumption that all parties of the interaction are *allies* who look for ways to support one another and are committed to working together for their mutual success and the success of the organization.

There is a fundamental difference between this kind of interaction and the kinds of interactions that happen at Levels One and Two (and, in many places, at Level Three). Teams in Level Four organizations start as high-performing, collaborative partnerships instead of being characterized by guarded, testing, and often combative interactions.

Leaders throughout the organization no longer see interaction safety as "soft stuff" that is disconnected from the work of the organization. In fact, they see that more ideas are shared, which leads to retention of talent, greater speed to market, efficiencies in process, and improvements in quality.

As people feel safer to speak up, fewer mistakes are made. Problems are made visible and solved quickly. Meetings are productive spaces for sharing information, getting a 360-degree view of a problem, and making decisions. Time and energy are saved instead of wasted.

People start their workdays feeling energized and valued, expecting to contribute, ready to collaborate, open to new ideas, willing to share their thoughts, and excited to be part of the collective enterprise. They bring their full selves to work. At the end of their workdays, people might be physically tired, but they leave fulfilled and look forward to the next day's challenges and collaborations.

We walk into meetings ready to collaborate, knowing our colleagues have our backs.

Supported by the liberating, empowering sense of interaction safety, people share information freely and easily without barriers. They engage with each other in authentic interactions. They are willing to lean into discomfort and address conflicts and disagreements as gateways to creativity and inclusion.

People feel free to exchange ideas without fear of feeling judged. Interactions start with the assumption that those involved have trust. People work hard to maintain that trust by investing in one another.

Disrespectful actions and judgmental behaviors are seen as outside organizational norms and quickly challenged and stopped. Judging or unfairly challenging behaviors are recognized and pointed out with care and respect.

I am concerned not only with *my* interaction safety but also with *yours*.

People understand that everyone does not feel safe in every interaction, every day. People make it a point to ask their colleagues what they need to feel safe. They work together to create that environment.

Bridget loves her job, and she's not ashamed to say so!

Bridget is the best kind of ambassador for her company. Bridget's good friend Jamal asks her why she is so excited about her organization. "I love my work, my colleagues, and the environment. I feel respected, and I am doing great work. I never feel like I need to censor myself. When I share an idea, others build on it. Together, we are achieving great results and surpassing our competition. I feel creative and challenged every day.

"When new people join, we want to learn from them. We want to hear about areas for improvement that they are seeing with their fresh eyes.

"We have a really strong foundation of trust, and we assume others will bring value. We seek out others: Who is missing? Who needs to be included? What differences in perspective do we need to solve this problem?

"We have created an amazing environment in which we are all growing, learning, and doing better together than we would alone. And we know we need to keep working at it."

At Level Four, *these* kinds of interactions seem normal.

Are they "normal" in your organization?

▶ Human resources policies, practices, and management systems enhance and maintain a culture of interaction safety.

▶ Organizational values support a culture of interaction safety—candidness, trust, and transparency.

▶ People support one another's growth, build on one another's ideas, and enjoy doing their best work together.

▶ The culture is fun and exciting.

▶ Honest, authentic interactions are the norm.

▶ The environment encourages the search for diverse perspectives and information, leading to faster decision-making and problem solving. People are eager to have dialogue across differences and are skilled in doing so.

▶ When people are talking about organizational results, interaction safety is always a part of the discussion since it is so integrated into how results are achieved.

▶ New people are welcomed, listened to, and valued for their prior experiences and new perspectives.

▶ Leaders and team members are proactive in sustaining a culture of interaction safety.

▶ Checklists and check-ins for interaction safety are integrated into all practices, processes, and meetings. People feel safe interacting with others but don't take interaction safety for granted.

We expect the best of each other, and we support each other so each of us can be our best self, doing our best work together, and grow to become even better.

Interaction safety enables a stronger product.

By empowering others, Kristen finds she is reenergizing herself. Kristen is leading a meeting of her team and talking about a new initiative she created that she's excited about when one member raises his hand and questions an underlying assumption. Another member agrees and suggests a significant change to Kristen's plan. She reacts well. Kristen checks her immediate impulse to reject the assertion, stops, listens to their comments, asks for more, sees the wisdom of their additions, and adjusts the plan accordingly. The team members feel listened to and know they really added value. She recognizes that the end product is much stronger. And it all took minutes.

How We Interact in Meetings: Level Four

"Normal" behaviors, interactions, and responses

Written rules and road signs	People know and live the behaviors that create interaction safety.
When someone is talking	People listen supportively and find ways to add value and useful ideas to most, if not all, conversations.
Interactions with the meeting leader	Everyone is there to contribute or would not have been invited. People speak freely.
Interactions with other team members	Interaction safety with others is assumed. There is a trusting and open environment.
When someone challenges an idea	Actively engage others to hear their different points of view. Listen with curiosity.
Outcome of interactions	Creativity, faster problem solving, and breakthroughs are common. Trust, inclusion, and collaboration are the norm for higher performance.

New people are welcomed as untapped resources for fresh ideas and new perspectives.

They are encouraged to spread their wings and soar

. . . but sometimes shushed until they "learn the ropes."

Thinking about his new job, Hassan is tempted to pinch himself. Hassan is truly excited to be at his new job and new company. He smiles to himself, remembering that he always wanted to work with this company. He admired its great mission and products and was attracted to what he heard about its culture of trust, inclusion, and collaboration.

Throughout the interview process, Hassan could feel people's genuineness. The vibe was warm and sincere, and the interviewers showed interest in who he was as a person in addition to all he could bring to the company. He was impressed with the level of honesty and openness in his interactions with potential team members and also with the organization's leaders. People shared information with him not only about the job but also about their backgrounds and their hopes for and concerns about the organization. They were real and forthcoming.

As Hassan thinks about his new position, he realizes he is a bit overwhelmed by the level of authority and empowerment he has, but he feels well supported by his new colleagues and leaders, who have made it clear they will help him navigate his learning curve. Best of all, he has already been able to contribute and his ideas have been welcomed.

Colleagues have said they want him to bring his perspectives to the table. What an exciting way to start! The future here looks bright.

Now it's time for that lunch meeting with his colleagues, a mandatory part of on-boarding. Hassan knows that taking the time to build connections with others is a critical part of creating trust and interaction safety. He can't wait to see what he and his new teammates are able to accomplish together.

 People who don't fit the traditional profile for employees in other organizations often feel very much at home, for the first time.

Jayden found an old folder with his resume in it, and he starts to think . . . He has been working at the organization for more than five years, longer than he's worked anywhere else. Jayden is surprised he's been here this long, and he reflects on why. This organization and its environment are so different from any other place he has been.

In the past, Jayden felt he was often treated differently from others because of his race. But in this organization, people value all he has to bring—not just his different perspectives and technical skills but also his potential.

Jayden is surrounded by diverse team members. His team is a mix of races, genders, national origins, sexual orientations, gender identities, religions, and styles. There is so much diversity that Jayden no longer feels as though he stands out as an individual, as he has in other organizations. Everyone stands out, and that is valued. Having that diversity has enabled the team to be innovative, opening up new markets, developing new products, and designing new services for customers. It's a great place to work and engage with others.

"Why would I want to leave?" he thinks.

Soaring Higher

Here are some everyday actions to help you soar higher.

You can only achieve Level Four by working to achieve and sustain it every day.

Individual Actions: Taking Risks

☑ Don't take interaction safety for granted. Check in with new and existing team members on what they need for interaction safety.

☑ Practice the 4 Keys for teamwork and collaboration: Listen as an Ally, Lean into Discomfort, State Your Intent and Intensity, and Share Your Street Corner.

☑ Address conflicts when they arise.

☑ Share your ideas and observations about needs and opportunities for enhancing interaction safety in the organization with team members and leaders.

☑ Keep raising the bar on interaction safety.

Leader and Organization Actions

☑ Model the behaviors and attitudes needed to create interaction safety.

☑ Ensure new leaders are coached and developed to practice interaction safety behaviors.

- ✓ Review and conduct listening tours to ensure interaction safety continues to be a foundational part of the culture.

- ✓ Make sure creating interaction safety is a skill requirement that is included in performance reviews and compensation discussions for all organizational leaders.

- ✓ Continue to assess how the organization is doing in regard to interaction safety.

- ✓ Involve new hires early in their employment and involve social identity groups regarding how they are experiencing interaction safety and areas for improvement.

- ✓ Recognize the need to refresh and reinvigorate the focus on interaction safety for continuous improvement.

- ✓ Continue to share examples of how interaction safety is impacting individual, team, and organizational performance.

An Invitation

Are You Ready?

We know what we have presented in this book, especially Level Four, may seem like a fairy tale. And we know it is possible—we have seen interaction safety in practice. Even better, we have seen the results—the collaboration, the innovation, the way people and teams are unleashed, and the higher organization performance. When interaction safety is a Way of Life, the energy people used to spend walking on eggshells, trying to get their ideas heard, navigating minefields, or avoiding those they distrust can instead be put toward doing their best work and winning bigger for the organization—speaking up, being big, and reaching out to make connections to innovate and solve problems in ways that aren't possible in an environment of fear and distrust.

A Level Three or Four organization creates space and room for people to make mistakes and truly collaborate together.

When interaction safety is present, conflict doesn't go away—it takes on a different shape, one that is not win-lose but an opportunity for growth and learning. The focus is on the goal of creating and maintaining interaction safety for all. All people strive to walk toward their talk and achieve a vision of an organization in which interaction safety is the norm.

That doesn't mean getting there is easy. People must be willing to be vulnerable, let go of past experiences, and *take a leap*—to be big, brave, and bold with others and be willing to step into a new realm of interaction with one another. It takes the dedication and commitment of leaders and team members who understand interaction safety is a fundamental component of unleashing creativity and higher performance.

So Where Do You Start?

To get to interaction safety, you first need to be clear about what interaction safety means to you. What are the behaviors that support your own feelings of interaction safety? What are the things you already do to help others feel safe, and what other behaviors can you practice to create a sense of safety for yourself and others? Make an individual commitment to be more conscious of your mind-sets and behaviors, and identify one to two actions you can do more of or start doing to build that safety. In Appendix I we identify seven core steps you, your team members, and the organization can take to move to deeper levels of trust, inclusion, and collaboration, which will facilitate movement through the levels of interaction safety. We also identify some of the key dos and don'ts to help you get started.

We know safety goes beyond our own actions and feelings, though. Think about a person in your life with whom you feel safe to be your full self, a person who supports you (even when that means giving you hard feedback), a person with whom you can be open and honest and not worry about having to be perfect. This might be a family member, a best friend, or maybe even a team member. Think about what makes those interactions safe—how they listen, how you exchange ideas. Consider the mind-sets you bring into those interactions and the language you use.

You might be thinking, *These are the people I trust most. How am I supposed to get that with people I work with?* Our advice is to start where you have the most trust and interaction safety already—the team members you trust the most. Have a conversation with them about what you are thinking. Ask what *they* need to feel safe, because their needs are likely not the same as yours. Share what makes you feel safe, along with what you have learned from this book about the behaviors that support interaction safety. Commit to ways you will support one another in creating that environment of safety. These don't have to be monumental actions—don't take on the biggest challenges or the least safe situations first. Start where you have support. Look for opportunities to create small wins and build some success. The first steps might be as simple as chiming in with support or encouragement when a colleague shares an idea. Think about where your organization is and use the suggestions for action in this book to guide your next steps or help identify the behaviors you want to practice.

As you begin testing the waters with those you trust, think about how you can expand your circle of interaction safety. Are there leaders with whom you can broach this subject? What about members of your team? Begin building a group of allies and encourage them to think about their own needs for interaction safety, as well as how they might put some of these behaviors into practice too.

Not everyone will be immediately supportive of creating interaction safety. A common refrain we have heard from leaders is "I have a business to run—I don't have time to coddle people with this soft stuff." Yes, it takes time to slow down and consider what people need to have interaction safety and work toward building it. However, given the possibilities interaction safety unlocks, we think the time and effort aren't just beneficial—they're necessary. Most leaders would never say, "We don't have time to ensure we are complying with industry regulations," or, "We don't have time to baby people with safety equipment before doing dangerous work." We don't know of many organizations that can afford anything less than the best work from every person. Today's organizations need everyone to work together to address and solve problems. And we know organizations can't get people's best thinking if they are too afraid to even share those ideas. We know there are naysayers out there with good reasons and powerful experiences that make them doubt that interaction safety in a Level Four workplace is possible. Some leaders believe the way to hold on to their power is to always be the smartest person in the room, and they therefore feel threatened by the idea of people speaking up. Some still operate with a "my way or the highway" mind-set. We have worked in organizations where such old-school behaviors among some leaders have instilled enough fear in people that they have learned to hold back important information or thinking, where people have been beaten down by daily insults and have been hurt too many times to be willing to trust once more.

We know greater interaction safety is needed in *every* organization. And we know it is possible! We have seen it and experienced it—perhaps not a whole organization at Level Four but certainly many islands at Level Three.

Interaction safety for all is the new frontier for human beings to be their best and bring their best to every interaction and, in turn, create higher performance and higher contributions.

We invite you to begin this journey if you haven't already. And to continue it if you have—to accelerate it! Find one person with whom you can establish a level of interaction safety. Then another and another. Be the leader people trust and encourage your colleagues to do the same. Implement practices and policies that support interaction safety in everything you do.

Are you ready? It's time to make it safe enough to soar!

Appendix I

Seven Steps to Creating Interaction Safety

Steps

1. Make it clear in your interactions with team members that greater interaction safety is your goal.

2. Assess what level of interaction safety currently exists (most of the time) and identify actions needed to move to the next level.

3. Ask each person what she or he needs for greater interaction safety.

4. Share and adopt the dos and don'ts and add others that would be helpful to you and the team.

5. Get agreement on where you want to be and how you will support each other.

6. Start practicing the new behaviors for greater interaction safety.

7. Assess how you are doing on an ongoing basis; celebrate what you are doing well, and continuously improve.

Dos and Don'ts for Interaction Safety

DOS	DON'TS
Join	Judge
Yes, and . . .	Yes, but . . .
Encourage	Belittle
Find agreement	Find holes
Be supportive	Be skeptical
Challenge for learning or growth and add value	Challenge to one-up others
Assume and extend trust	Withhold trust
Initiate	Hold back
Be open and available	Be cautious
Express yourself	Second-guess yourself
Problem solve	Find blame

Appendix II
Assessment

Where Are You? Where Is Your Organization?

How We Interact in Meetings: "Normal" behaviors, interactions, and responses

	Level One On Your Own	Level Two Lip Service
Written rules and road signs	There are no statements about the importance of interaction safety.	Signs about interaction safety are posted but not followed.
When someone is talking	Keep your head down. Wait your turn to talk. Or judge and poke holes in what the person has said.	People listen when it is something that directly relates to them. Mostly, people just wait for the pause that means it's their turn to speak.
Interactions with the meeting leader	It is the leader's meeting. Only speak when spoken to.	Comment (guardedly) when you have something important to say.
Interactions with other team members	Only interact with other team members when absolutely necessary. Protect yourself and your team from being belittled.	State agreements in meetings. State disagreements privately with those you feel safe with.
When someone challenges an idea	Go on the attack or avoid interaction.	Calculate the risk of responding. Talk to others rather than directly to the individual.
Outcome of interactions	Interactions are passive-aggressive. Time and energy are wasted. There is no trust, inclusion, or collaboration.	Performance is suboptimal, problems are not fully explored, and all points of view do not come forward. There is little trust, inclusion, or collaboration.

Level Three Islands of Safety	Level Four Way of Life
Signs in the room promote interaction safety. Some individuals and teams refer to them a lot, others not at all.	People know and live the behaviors that create interaction safety.
People test whether this is a group in which interaction safety is a norm and respond accordingly.	People listen supportively and find ways to add value and useful ideas to most, if not all, conversations.
People hold an expectation that they have something to offer. Everyone expects to, and is expected to, contribute.	Everyone is there to contribute or would not have been invited. People speak freely.
Interactions are free, open, and supportive. People know the ideal is not yet a reality everywhere and so they are sometimes cautious.	Interaction safety with others is assumed. There is a trusting and open environment.
The norm is to listen and try to see the other's point of view. Disrespectful challenges are rare and usually called out.	Actively engage others to hear their different point of view. Listen with curiosity.
Uneven levels of skill and commitment lead to uneven outcomes. There are islands of trust, inclusion, collaboration, and high performance.	Creativity, faster problem solving, and breakthroughs are common. Trust, inclusion, and collaboration are the norm for higher performance.

Acknowledgments

This book would not have been possible without the many people who partnered with us to make it happen.

First and foremost, once again, thank you to our dear friend Roger Gans for your partnership and brilliance in making our work soar. We appreciate all the support you have given and work you have done from the inception of this project to make it a reality—all while writing a dissertation! Thank you from our hearts for your collaboration, availability, and brilliance—always a treat. Tara Whittle, thank you for your insights and dedication to helping us bring forth our best. It is always good to have a *Jeopardy* contestant on the team. And a special thanks to Katelyn Kasmier for keeping us organized as we have gone through the many drafts of this book and the late nights and marathon writing sessions.

Thank you, Deborah Dagit and Harold L. Yoh III, for writing the forewords for this book. You are friends and leaders who are living interaction safety as you bring diversity, inclusion, and safer work environments to organizations. We are honored to know you and to get to hang out with you.

Mickey Bradley and Monica Biggs, two The Kaleel Jamison Consulting Group, Inc. consultants, your insights and experience enhanced the book because of your thinking, wealth of consulting experience, and honest feedback. Thank you!

We thank our many colleagues and friends who added their thinking, responded to our many questions and surveys about the book, and were a continued source of support and caring for us throughout this process—Glenn Bates, Kathy Clements, Dennis DaRos, Katelyn Kasmier, Daniel Levine, David Levine, Pauline Kamen Miller, Cindy Szadokierski, Andrew Van Breugel, Alison VanDerVolgen, Ilene Wasserman, and Harold L. Yoh III. Everyone helped make the book better, and we hope we did justice to your suggestions. We would also like to thank the many people who helped us select the title for this book. Your contributions are greatly appreciated. And a big thank-you goes to the Berrett-Koehler reviewers, who provided lengthy feedback to move the initial draft to new levels—Valerie Andres, Mike McNair, Joseph A. Webb, and Leigh Wilkinson.

Safe Enough to Soar would not be a book without our longtime editor, Steve Piersanti. Thank you, Steve, for your brilliance in assisting us to find the core of our message, challenging us as an ally, and believing in us and our work in the world. A *big* thank-you goes to Jeevan Sivasubramaniam for the many roles you played in the creation of this book. Once again you have brought energy to the book with your wonderful artwork. We love the bean people. Thanks for bringing them to life again. Thanks, Edward Wade, for managing the layout and many other aspects of this book. And thank you, Mimi Heft, for bringing your creativity to our manuscript and bringing it to life through your layout and artistic touch. We also appreciate María Jesús Aguiló, Shabnam Banerjee-McFarland, Leslie Crandell, Michael Crowley, Kristen Frantz, Catherine Lengronne, Liz McKellar, Melody Negron, Anders Renee, Courtney Schonfeld, Katie Sheehan, Johanna Vondeling, Lasell Whipple, and Chloe Wong. And to the whole Berrett-Koehler team: you are great, and we love working with you. The Berrett-Koehler community of staff and authors is a special and precious community, and we are so very proud to be part of it for this, our fourth book.

And, finally, thank you to everyone in The Kaleel Jamison Consulting Group, Inc. Business Village. You inspire us, nudge us to be better, and support us at every step on every journey. We do our founder, who started our company forty-eight years ago, proud. We feel Kaleel's smile as we work together to make this a better world for all. And, last and most important, thanks to our clients, both current and past. You always teach us. We are so honored and proud to partner with you to make your organizations and this world a better place. We learn so much from you every day.

To all of those we mentioned and those we may have forgotten: thank you for enabling us to soar— and to achieve something that we could not have done without you.

About the Authors

Frederick A. Miller and Judith H. Katz

For more than thirty years, Fred and Judith have been working individually and together to transform organizations and the ways people interact with one another within them.

They started their business partnership in 1985, Judith coming from faculty positions at the University of Oklahoma and San Diego State, and Fred from management positions at Connecticut General Life Insurance Company. It was a major turning point in both their lives.

As, respectively, CEO and executive vice president for The Kaleel Jamison Consulting Group, Inc.— one of *Consulting* magazine's Seven Small Jewels in 2010—they have partnered with Fortune 100 and other companies, universities, governmental agencies, municipalities, and nonprofit organizations to create organizations in which the level of interaction safety elevates the quality of interactions, leverages people's differences, and transforms workplaces into growth-and-learning environments where people's talents are unleashed, results are accelerated, and productivity soars. Their partnership is proof that teamwork and collaboration do create breakthroughs.

Through their thought leadership and practical approaches for changing workplaces, they have brought their unique perspectives, passion, and energy to make a difference in organizations that few can match.

In addition to this book and many other writings, together they have also coauthored the following:

▶ *Opening Doors to Teamwork and Collaboration: 4 Keys That Change Everything* (2013)

▶ *Be BIG: Step Up, Step Out, Be Bold* (2008)

▶ *The Inclusion Breakthrough: Unleashing the Real Power of Diversity* (2002)

Judith and Fred have each been honored with several of their field's most distinguished awards. In 2007, *Profiles in Diversity Journal* named them two of forty Pioneers of Diversity, and in 2012, they were both honored as Legends of Diversity by the International Society of Diversity and Inclusion Professionals. Among other awards they have received are Fred's Lifetime Achievement Award and Service to the Network Award, presented by the Organization Development Network (ODN), and the Winds of Change Award from the Forum on Workplace Inclusion. Judith has received ODN's Lifetime Achievement Award, the Outstanding Achievement in Global Work Award, and the award for Communicating OD (Organizational Development) Knowledge, as well as the Cultural Competency Award from Diversity Training University

International. Fred has served on Ben and Jerry's and Day & Zimmermann's corporate boards. Judith is currently a member of the Fielding Graduate University Board of Trustees and has served on Social Venture Network's and National Training Laboratories Institute's boards, as well as on the University of Massachusetts Dean's Leadership Council.

Their consulting practice, workshops, and conference presentations have impacted clients and groups in the United States, Singapore, India, China, Japan, Thailand, the United Kingdom, Australia, the Netherlands, and Mexico.

Judith loves fishing and traveling with David, her husband.

Fred is a workaholic who loves being at home with his marriage partner, Pauline, and the fancy guppies that he raises.

Judith's extraversion and Fred's introversion often cause them to see the world from different street corners, which has led to many intense conversations, personal and professional revelations—and a lot of laughter and creativity.

Through their work together, they have been able, individually and collectively, to soar—and to inspire and enable other individuals, teams, and organizations to do the same.

Berrett–Koehler
Publishers

Berrett-Koehler is an independent publisher dedicated to an ambitious mission: *Connecting people and ideas to create a world that works for all.*

We believe that the solutions to the world's problems will come from all of us, working at all levels: in our organizations, in our society, and in our own lives. Our BK Business books help people make their organizations more humane, democratic, diverse, and effective (we don't think there's any contradiction there). Our BK Currents books offer pathways to creating a more just, equitable, and sustainable society. Our BK Life books help people create positive change in their lives and align their personal practices with their aspirations for a better world.

All of our books are designed to bring people seeking positive change together around the ideas that empower them to see and shape the world in a new way.

And we strive to practice what we preach. At the core of our approach is Stewardship, a deep sense of responsibility to administer the company for the benefit of all of our stakeholder groups including authors, customers, employees, investors, service providers, and the communities and environment around us. Everything we do is built around this and our other key values of quality, partnership, inclusion, and sustainability.

This is why we are both a B-Corporation and a California Benefit Corporation—a certification and a for-profit legal status that require us to adhere to the highest standards for corporate, social, and environmental performance.

We are grateful to our readers, authors, and other friends of the company who consider themselves to be part of the BK Community. We hope that you, too, will join us in our mission.

A BK Business Book

We hope you enjoy this BK Business book. BK Business books pioneer new leadership and management practices and socially responsible approaches to business. They are designed to provide you with groundbreaking and practical tools to transform your work and organizations while upholding the triple bottom line of people, planet, and profits. High-five!

To find out more, visit **www.bkconnection.com**.

Berrett–Koehler
Publishers

Connecting people and ideas
to create a world that works for all

Dear Reader,

Thank you for picking up this book and joining our worldwide community of Berrett-Koehler readers. We share ideas that bring positive change into people's lives, organizations, and society.

To welcome you, we'd like to offer you a free e-book. You can pick from among twelve of our bestselling books by entering the promotional code BKP92E here: http://www .bkconnection.com/welcome.

When you claim your free e-book, we'll also send you a copy of our e-newsletter, the BK Communiqué. Although you're free to unsubscribe, there are many benefits to sticking around. In every issue of our newsletter you'll find

- A free e-book
- Tips from famous authors
- Discounts on spotlight titles
- Hilarious insider publishing news
- A chance to win a prize for answering a riddle

Best of all, our readers tell us, "Your newsletter is the only one I actually read." So claim your gift today, and please stay in touch!

Sincerely,

Charlotte Ashlock
Steward of the BK Website

Questions? Comments?
Contact me at bkcommunity@bkpub.com.